# Because You Exist



Aesira

# Dedication

*For the one who stayed,*
*even when I was too much.*

# Preface

It began with wanting more than I was given. I thought it might grow into a relationship if I was patient. It didn't, and that took time to accept.

But the feeling didn't disappear. It changed.

What I feel now is quieter. It doesn't pull at me the way it used to. I no longer hope for something different. I no longer focus on what it is not. I am grateful that he is in my life, and that we share what we do.

These poems were written during that shift. Some come from when I still wanted more. Others were written when I began to understand that love does not always need to become a relationship to have value.

We never became a couple. There was no clear turning point. Just time, and the realization that having him in my life as a companion is enough.

# Acknowledgment

To *Kit*,

This book exists because of you. You stayed on the phone on nights I couldn't be alone. You answered even when neither of us really had the right words. You sang when you didn't know how to comfort me. You probably thought it was small, but it wasn't.

A lot of these poems were written after we hung up, or in the quiet spaces between conversations. I don't think you realize how much those moments mattered to me.

Thank you for staying, for your patience when I made things harder. For showing up even when you were tired. For being there when it would've been easier to step back.

There are pieces of you all through this book. In the loud parts, in the softer ones, and in the background hum of a call that didn't fix everything but made it feel lighter.

This is for you.

# 1. Someone I've never Held

Your name is etched into me so deeply
I can hear it with every heartbeat.

My chest aches each morning
When I wake and find no trace of you beside
me.

How foolish of me,
To crave something I've never touched,
To miss someone I've never held.

I look for you in every crowd.
And when I'm alone,
The emptiness screams louder than silence.

I haven't met you yet,
But somehow,
You already live in
Every corner of me.

## 2. The Window

It hurts
To want something
So quietly,
so desperately.

Like watching sunlight
Spill through a window
You can never open.

To reach
Again and again
Knowing your hands
Will never be enough
To hold it.

To ache in silence,
while the world keeps turning
As if your heart
Isn't breaking
In the stillness.

And still
You keep looking at it,
Keep hoping, that
Maybe someday
It'll reach back.

Loving you
will never be a burden,
even when it hurts.

# 3. Every Line I Write

We might not have been
But you,
You live in every line I write.

In the pauses between words,
In the ache of the what ifs.

In the soft,
desperate longing
Of what could have been.

There's a piece of you
Tucked inside every poem,
Every silence I've filled
With the things I never said.

I never thought
I'd write about love.

But now my pages bleed
With secret confessions.

Maybe
one day,
you'll find them.
Maybe you'll read them.
Then you'll know
Just how much
I loved you.

# 4. On Speaker

I didn't need you to talk.
I didn't even know what I would say
if you did.

I just didn't want
the silence to be louder than me.

You said you'd stay.
You didn't ask how long.
Just left the phone on speaker
so I wouldn't feel alone,
even if you fell asleep.

I stared at the ceiling
Listened to nothing
And everything.

Your breathing,
The fan
The rustle of the sheets.

At some point,
My body stopped bracing
My breathing  matched yours
And for the first time in days,
I slept.

## 5. Aftercare

You tell me
to drink water
before asking how I feel,
like tending the body first
is what you do when words unreal.

Sit down.
Breathe slow.
Put the sharp things away.

You stay for the moment
where I might start to fray,
until the room feels quieter,
until my thoughts obey.

Then you leave without ceremony,
without needing any praise,
trusting I'll be alright
once the storm finds its way.

# 6. Cotton Candy

We don't usually talk like that.
You don't like calls.
You say they take too much out of you.

But that day,
You wanted to talk.
And hearing your voice
felt like coming home.

It felt like
sunlight finding you
on a slow morning.
Like cotton candy
melting on my tongue.

Like a blanket pulled up
on a night colder than expected.

Your laugh
caught me off guard
The way familiar comfort does.

Like tasting something you love
after forgetting how good it is.

I didn't think about it much then
But later I realized
how light everything felt
While I could hear your voice.

# 7. You Never Raise Your Hand

You help me so graciously,
yet you speak of your own anxiety
like talk of the weather.

You don't ask to be held,
nor do you wait long enough
to see if someone might try.

You survive quietly and alone
and still say you lack strength.

I wonder how much of you
goes unseen
just because you never raise your hand.

# 8. I Hear You

It's stupid how one text
can make my breathing feel lighter.
How a voice note
can calm the chaos in my head.

Nothing actually changes.
The storm is still there.
But somehow
I'm not standing in it alone.

People have always told me
I feel too much.
Want too deeply.
Break too easily.

He sees all of it
And he doesn't look away.

It's the small things.
How he stays.
How he waits.
How he says the right thing
without knowing
I needed it.

He listens.
Like my words matter.
=And even when I don't say anything,
he still hears me.

He never tells me
to be stronger.
Never says it's "just a phase."
He just says,
*"I hear you."*

And I don't know why
but hearing that
makes me hear myself again.

Not because he fixes me.

But because
he never asks me
to be fixed.

And somehow
when he holds me when I'm breaking,
I don't feel broken at all.

# 9. Whenever You're Ready

I won't ask you to talk.
Or smile.
Or let me in.

I'll stay here.
Quiet.
Unmoving.
The way the sky is.
Even when the curtains are drawn.

If the weight gets heavy
and the quiet gets cruel,
you don't have to explain.

Just come find me.
I won't ask anything.
But I'll sit with you
Until you can breathe again.

And even if you're never ready,
I'll still be here.

# 10. Let Someone Take Care of You

You hold on when no one else would.
You see through the cracks
and hear what goes unspoken.

You give your time,
your words,
your care
without asking for anything in return.

You are a soul that makes the world lighter,
even without trying,
lifting others even when you're tired,
listening even when no one listens to you.

I hope life is gentle with you.
I hope you receive
all the little things you've ever wished for.

Peace
Love
Care
The same gifts
you give so freely to everyone else.

And I hope, one day,
you let someone take care of you too.
Because you deserve it.
Maybe more than anyone I know.

## 11. Just Once

I won't pretend I didn't hope.
Even when I knew,
deep down,
how this would end.

At first, I thought it was passing,
a momentary spark,
something that would fade.
But it grew,
too fast.

I've never wanted someone this much.
Never ached so much to be seen,
and maybe loved.

You said you're not looking for a
relationship.

But I remember
you once said you wanted one.
So maybe
it's just not with me.

And that's okay.
Not painless,
but okay.

So I'll try.
To let it go.
To keep the friendship
and bury the rest.

But before I do,
just once,
let me say it.

*I love you.*
Not to change your mind.
Or to make it harder.

But, so those words
don't die unheard.

# 12. If You Asked

You say you don't believe
anyone can love you.
But I chose to stay.
I chose to keep living
for you, my love.

When my soul wants nothing but an end,
when surviving feels harder than leaving,
I still try
because you asked me to.

What more proof do you need
than that?

I won't talk about grand gestures
or impossible promises.
But if you asked for me,
I'd be there
without thinking twice.

You can't believe
anyone could love you.
And here I am,
unable to understand
how anyone ever couldn't.

# 13. In Between

I feel guilty for surviving
after all the things I said.
It makes me wonder
if everyone thinks
I only cried out for attention.

But I know the truth.
It wasn't for show.

I don't want to die
if it means breaking you.
I don't want to live
if it means breaking myself.

So I stay stuck in-between
breathing, hurting,
ashamed of both.

And maybe that's why
I always stop myself.
Not because
I don't want the ending,

but because the thought of causing you
pain
hurts more than the thoughts in my
head.

So I survive another night,
with a tired heart.
Trying not to hurt
the one person who would care
if I was gone.

## 14. You Don't Know This

You don't know this,
but there were nights
I only made it through
because you were on the other end
of a quiet line.

You don't know this,
but the way you say
"I'm here"
has more weight
than most promises I've been given.

You think you're ordinary.
Like it wasn't anything.
Like anyone would have done the same.

They wouldn't have.

You listened longer than you needed to.
You stayed longer than you had to.
But even staying
is not small.

And maybe you don't see it,
but I do.

I remember.

Because of you,
I breathe a little easier.
Hope a little louder.
And want to stay
just a little longer.

So thank you for hearing
what I couldn't say,
for staying beside me
when others walked away.

# 15. I Won't Make You Stay

I learned how to care for you
without asking you to stay.
I'm learning how to sit with the longing
and not turn it into a request.

I won't hold you tighter
when you pull away.
I won't ask questions
that sound like traps.

This time,
If you leave,
I'll let you.

And if you stay,
I hope it's not because I begged you to.

What if loving me
is like sleeping next to a nightmare?

# 16. Lighthouse

I used to reach for you
with both hands open,
as if hearing you
could make my lungs
remember how to work.

Now
I'm learning
to sit with my own shaking.

You don't know
how often I practice
being okay
before I speak to you.
How I rewrite sentences
so they don't sound like
"please don't go."

How I swallow the parts of me
that want to make you
a lighthouse.

I still fail,
many times.

But I know
you are not a lighthouse.
You are a person
with dinner plates in your hands,
noise in your house,
and storms I cannot see.

And still,
you show up.
You have helped me
in ways you do not measure.

I am trying to build
my own floor now.

So when I stand beside you,
it is not because
I would collapse without you.
It is because
I choose to.

Still learning that
care can be quiet,
that distance is not disappearance,
that a pause is not a verdict.

## 17. Because You Exist

Someone asked me today
why I love you so much.
Why I don't move on
when you don't feel the same.

I laughed,
because how do you explain
something that was never a transaction?

Why should love need permission?
Why should it exist only
if it's returned?

If I loved you for a reason,
wouldn't that make it fragile?
Something that disappears
the moment the reason does?

I don't believe in that kind of love.
At least, not for me.

I love you without conditions.
Without bargains.
I love you because you exist,
because you are who you are.

And even if you changed,
even if the world wore you down
or broke you into someone new,
I know this much
would stay the same.

I still find you
in moments you don't belong in.

In ordinary days
where everything I do
has quietly learned your name.

9 789357 733007

Printed at Repro India Ltd.